BASEBALL >>
SEASON TICKET
THE ULTIMATE FAN GUIDE

D1521735

BY DOUG WILLIAMS

First Edition
First Printing, 2019

Book design by Sarah Taplin
Cover design by Sarah Taplin
Photographs ©: Patrick Gorski/Icon Sportswire/AP Images, cover (top); David Lee/ Shutterstock Images, cover (center background); Kyodo/AP Images, cover (bottom left); Tom Gannam/AP Images, cover (bottom right top); Eric Christian Smith/AP Images, cover (bottom right bottom); Ezra Shaw/Getty Images, 4, 11, 30; Mark Rucker/Transcendental Graphics/Getty Images, 9, 62–63, 72; Jose Luis Villegas/Sacramento Bee/MCT/Tribune News Service/Getty Images, 12; George Grantham Bain Collection/Library of Congress, 15; Nick Laham/Getty Images, 18; Jonathan Daniel/Getty Images, 20–21; Bettmann/Getty Images, 22, 26, 43, 47, 64, 68, 76, 79; Christopher Pasatieri/Getty Images, 29; Christian Petersen/Getty Images, 33, 56; Stanley Weston/Getty Images, 36-37; Rick Stewart/ Allsport/Getty Images, 39; Marty Lederhandler/AP Images, 40; Focus on Sport/Getty Images, 48, 53, 60; Sporting News/Getty Images, 55; AP Images, 67; Wayne Kryduba/ Minnesota Twins/Getty Images, 70–71; Matthew Sharpe/WireImage, 80; Scott Halleran/ Getty Images, 83; Greg Nelson/Sports Illustrated/Getty Images, 84; Jim McIsaac/Getty Images, 87; Jeff Gross/Getty Images, 88; Otto Greule Jr/Getty Images, 92; Elsa/Getty Images, 95; Red Line Editorial, 96–97

Design Elements ©: Shutterstock Images

Press Box Books, an imprint of Press Room Editions

Library of Congress Control Data Number: 2018940603

ISBN:
978-1-63494-034-4 (paperback)
978-1-63494-039-9 (epub)
978-1-63494-044-3 (hosted ebook)

Distributed by North Star Editions, Inc.
2297 Waters Drive
Mendota Heights, MN 55120
www.northstareditions.com

Printed in the United States of America

TABLE OF CONTENTS

CHAPTER 1

AMERICA'S PASTIME

Chicago Cubs third baseman Kris Bryant started smiling as soon as the ground ball was hit his way. Even as he fielded the ball and threw to first base, Bryant was grinning. A moment later, so was every Cubs fan in America.

Bryant's throw with two outs in the bottom of the 10th inning gave the Cubs the World Series championship after a wait of 108 years. On the rainy night of November 2, 2016, they pulled off an 8–7 victory over the Indians in Game 7 at Cleveland's Progressive Field. The extra inning added even more drama to one of baseball's most long-awaited stories.

Kris Bryant celebrates as the Cubs clinch their first World Series win in 108 years.

The Cubs' last World Series championship had come in 1908. Generations of fans had gone their entire lives without seeing their beloved Cubbies win the big one. While baseball flourished and evolved through two world wars, 18 US presidents, and the dawning of a new century, the Cubs were baseball's franchise of futility. Some said they were cursed.

> 66 I'm just so happy for Cubs fans over the last 108 years, generations, some still here, some not. They were all here tonight. Everybody who's ever put on a Cubs uniform, this is for you."
> –Cubs general manager Theo Epstein

At long last, Cubs fans could share their joy with parents, grandparents, and even long-departed loved ones. Outside the Cubs' Wrigley Field, one fan had dedicated a brick to his grandfather. It read, "In heaven and still waiting." The day after the Cubs' victory, he added the words, "Not anymore."

"I'm just so happy for Cubs fans over the last 108 years, generations, some still here, some not," said Cubs general manager Theo Epstein. "They were all here tonight. Everybody who's ever put on a Cubs uniform, this is for you."

The Cubs' story in 2016 was special, but it's just a part of the game's rich history. More than any other sport, baseball's roots run deep in American culture. For most of the 20th century, baseball was the nation's favorite professional sport.

In 1924 President Calvin Coolidge called baseball "our national game." Former US president Herbert Hoover once said, "Next to religion, baseball has furnished a greater impact on American life than any other institution." During World War II (1939–1945), President Franklin D. Roosevelt asked Major League Baseball (MLB) to keep playing to take Americans' minds off the war.

The game has been a favorite subject of movies and books, from *Field of Dreams* to *Moneyball*. Standouts such as Babe Ruth and Joe DiMaggio had more star power than actors and entertainers. Baseball's language is universal. Success is a home run. Failure is a strikeout.

Change is a constant in America, but baseball has been a consistent thread joining the 19th, 20th, and 21st centuries. That's not to say baseball never changes, though.

The sport's popularity grew in parts of the United

States in the early 1800s. By the start of the Civil War in 1861, soldiers on both sides knew the game and played it when they had time. Even President Abraham Lincoln participated in games on the White House lawn. After the war, the game spread as returning soldiers took it to their homes. Rural towns and big cities alike soon had teams for what was called "base ball" or "town ball."

In its early years, the game was far different than it is now. Players didn't wear gloves or mitts. Fielders could get an out by hitting a base runner with a thrown ball. Pitchers were required to throw underhand. Batters could ask for a high or low pitch. For a while, too, players could use bats that were flat on one side.

In 1869 the Cincinnati Red Stockings (now the Reds) became the first pro team. They toured the country to play local amateurs. In 1876 the Red Stockings were part of the eight-team National League of Professional Baseball Clubs, today's National League (NL). In 1901 the American League (AL), also with eight teams, came along. Two years later, the champions of each league met in the first World Series, with the Boston Americans (now Red Sox) beating the Pittsburgh Pirates.

Born before football and basketball, baseball

Fans pour onto the field at Boston's Huntington Avenue Grounds during the 1903 World Series between the Boston Americans and Pittsburgh Pirates.

had everyone's attention. Kids played it, and adults flocked to ballparks as fans. In the early 1900s, the game was dominated by pitching, contact hitters, and base running. It was the "dead-ball era," when the handmade balls couldn't be hit far. Games often were low scoring and decided by bunting, stealing, and well-placed singles.

As 1920 approached, that changed. Machine-made balls traveled farther when hit. Home runs brought more excitement, and nobody created more of it than

9

Babe Ruth. The "Bambino" set the single-season record of 29 home runs in 1919, and hit 54 and 59 the next two seasons.

Baseball's evolution continued. The all-white major leagues finally admitted black players in 1947. In the 1950s, the majors moved west, with the New York Giants and Brooklyn Dodgers shifting to San Francisco and Los Angeles, respectively. Six waves of expansion from 1961 through 1998 put teams into new cities, and the major leagues expanded from 16 to 30 teams. Radio, television, and the Internet extended the sport's reach to every corner of the country.

Baseball has added night games, a designated hitter, and talent from around the world. Now it pays its best players millions of dollars. It has also been criticized for its slow pace of play and not connecting with young fans. Yet major league fans remain loyal.

In 2017 major league attendance was close to 73 million. The Cubs' victory over the Indians in Game 7 of the 2016 World Series attracted more than 40 million TV viewers.

Baseball has endured. Now a 19th-century game in the 21st century, millions of fans still love its history and strategy. Its slower pace allows fathers and

The 2016 Cubs celebrate their place in history after
winning the World Series.

daughters, and mothers and sons to savor it, talk about
it, and bond through it. And when their team wins a
championship, they celebrate together.

CHAPTER 2

PITCHING RULES THE GAME

There was little the Kansas City Royals could do. It was Game 1 of the 2014 World Series, and San Francisco Giants pitcher Madison Bumgarner was on fire. Mixing a four-seam fastball and a devastating curveball, the man nicknamed "MadBum" gave up just three hits and a run while striking out five batters in seven innings. The Giants won 7–1.

Five days later, Bumgarner was even better. He pitched all nine innings of a 5–0 victory and struck out eight. The Royals, the AL's second-best hitting team, were helpless against him. In Game 7, Bumgarner even came out of the bullpen to pitch five scoreless innings

Madison Bumgarner pitches for the Giants in Game 1 of the 2014 World Series.

and got the save in a 3–2 win. At one point he retired 14 straight batters. Most importantly, the victory gave the Giants their third World Series championship in five seasons.

In total, Bumgarner gave up just one run over 21 innings. He struck out 17 and had an earned run average (ERA) of 0.43. He was voted the Series' Most Valuable Player (MVP). Royals designated hitter Billy Butler said Bumgarner carried the Giants "on his back."

"He dominated every time he was on the mound," said Butler. "That's what true competitors and true aces do. That's what sets him apart from everybody else."

Bumgarner pitched his way into baseball history alongside so many other great starting pitchers, long known as aces. Dating to the late 1800s and early 1900s, when pitchers such as Cy Young and Charles "Old Hoss" Radbourn dominated opponents, baseball's aces have been rare and precious. A team with an ace can beat even the best hitting teams. There's a baseball saying: "Good pitching will always stop good hitting."

> " Pitching is No. 1. If your pitcher pitches a shutout, you can't lose."
> —Longtime Dodgers general manager Al Campanis

14

Denton Young earned the nickname Cy because he threw the ball so hard into a building that it looked like it had been hit by a cyclone.

"Pitching is No. 1," said longtime Los Angeles Dodgers general manager Al Campanis. "If your pitcher pitches a shutout, you can't lose."

Radbourn was a star of the early NL, winning 48 games in 1883 and 59 the next season. In 1884 he led the league in strikeouts, ERA, and innings pitched while completing 73 games. In that era, starting

15

pitchers rarely came out of a game. They also pitched more frequently than today's starting pitchers, who often take the mound every fifth day.

Denton True "Cy" Young was the pitching king. Young pitched 22 years in the major leagues. He retired in 1911 with 511 wins, the most in history. Five times he won more than 30 games. He was so esteemed that the annual award given to the best pitchers in the NL and AL is called the Cy Young Award.

The Baseball Hall of Fame inducted its first class in 1936. Pitchers Christy Mathewson and Walter Johnson were among the five inductees. Each had a style that made him terrific and popular.

Mathewson began with the New York Giants in 1900. His control and his famed screwball helped him compile a 373–188 record over his career. In the 1905 World Series, Mathewson pitched three shutouts over the Philadelphia Athletics. Many historians consider him to be the first great pitcher of the World Series era. He was also a role model for the way he acted on the field and off.

"He had knowledge, judgment, perfect control, and form," said Connie Mack, the Athletics' Hall of Fame manager. "It was wonderful to watch him pitch."

Johnson pitched his entire 21-year career with the Washington Senators and was known for his fastball. The great hitter Ty Cobb said Johnson's fastball made him flinch when it approached and "hissed with danger." Johnson, nicknamed "The Big Train," won 417 games. He held the career record for strikeouts when he retired in 1927.

The New York Yankees grew into a powerhouse in the 1920s. For decades they were known as the Bronx Bombers. But the Yankees also had some of the game's best pitchers. From Charles "Red" Ruffing to Ron Guidry, Vernon "Lefty" Gomez to Andy Pettitte, many Yankees aces rank among the best pitchers of their eras.

When the game changed in the 1970s to put more emphasis on relief pitching, the Yankees often had some of the best closers (pitchers who close out games and save victories). Lindy McDaniel, Sparky Lyle, Rich Gossage, and Dave Righetti were among the best. Mariano Rivera, however, was the best.

Rivera, who retired in 2013, pitched his entire 19-year career with the Yankees. He set major league records for saves, with 652, and added 42 saves in the postseason. Rivera mostly threw one pitch: a cutter.

Mariano Rivera's cutter was long one of the most feared pitches in baseball, especially among left-handed hitters.

The cutter is a fastball that breaks toward the opposite side. It helped Rivera, a right-hander, dominate, especially against left-handed hitters. Rivera helped the Yankees win five World Series by getting the tough outs late in games.

"He's the measuring stick for relievers, for greatness, for clutch performance," said Hall of Fame outfielder Reggie Jackson.

Even though relievers have become more important, ace starters have always held a glamour role. In the 1960s, Bob Gibson of the St. Louis Cardinals, Juan Marichal of the San Francisco Giants, and Sandy Koufax of the Dodgers were the elite. Injuries cut Koufax's career short, but he was incredible over his last five seasons. From 1962 to 1966 he went 111–34 and threw four no-hitters. His fastball and curveball were among the best of his era.

"Either he throws the fastest ball I've ever seen, or I'm going blind," said Hall of Fame outfielder Richie Ashburn.

Other aces have emerged in more recent years. Jim Palmer helped the Baltimore Orioles win championships in the 1960s, 1970s, and 1980s. Dwight Gooden took the New York Mets to a title in 1986.

> **Few pitchers in baseball history could bring the heat with their fastball quite like Nolan Ryan.**

Dennis Eckersley went from a good starter to a great closer to help the Oakland Athletics to the top in 1989.

And then there was Nolan Ryan. He won 324 games and broke the career strikeout record. He also pitched a record seven no-hitters. At age 44 in his 25th season

in 1991, Ryan was still throwing nearly 100 mph. When he threw his last no-hitter that season, Toronto Blue Jays manager Cito Gaston was in awe.

"Any time you face Nolan Ryan, two things can happen," he said. "He can beat you, or he can throw a no-hitter."

CHAPTER 3

THE BAMBINO CHANGES THE GAME

On the afternoon of April 18, 1923, more than 74,000 fans filled Yankee Stadium. It was the first official game at the new ballpark of the New York Yankees. The crowd was the largest in major league history. Fans wanted to be a part of something special, and their wishes came true.

The Yankees were leading the Boston Red Sox 1–0 in the bottom of the third inning when George Herman "Babe" Ruth came to bat. Ruth already was the greatest slugger the game had ever known.

No other player in baseball history had hit more than 29 home runs in a season when Babe Ruth hit 54 in 1920.

Just 28, the left-handed batter had already set the single-season record for home runs three times. He hit 29 for the Red Sox in 1919, breaking the existing mark of 27. After being sold to the Yankees in 1920, Ruth hit 54. In 1921 he hit 59. Now, fans were eager to see if Ruth and the Yankees were a fit for the new park.

With two Yankees on base, Ruth swung. The bat connected to send a line drive deep to right field that landed in the bleachers. The *New York Daily News* reporter covering the game described the blast as one of Ruth's best. It was hit so hard that it never "was over 30 feet from Earth." Just like that, the Yankees were up 4–0. They were on their way to a 98-win season and their first World Series championship. Ruth hit 41 home runs that season and was voted the AL's MVP. Yankee Stadium would forever be known as the "House that Ruth Built."

Ruth helped the Yankees become the best team in baseball during his career. He also was the game's biggest star. Wherever the Yankees played, fans bought tickets to watch Ruth hit the ball over the fence. He swung hard every at-bat. In his first season in New York, Yankees attendance nearly doubled.

Clearly, fans loved the way the game had changed from the earlier "dead-ball era." Then, scoring depended on singles, steals, and bunts. Now fans came out to see home runs and more scoring. Ruth's timing was perfect. He came along just as the cores of baseballs began to be machine made. The tighter cores were livelier and balls flew farther. Baseball became more popular than ever.

"He wasn't a baseball player," said Hall of Fame broadcaster Ernie Harwell. "He was a worldwide celebrity, an international star the likes of which baseball has never seen."

> ❝ He wasn't a baseball player. He was a worldwide celebrity, an international star the likes of which baseball has never seen."
>
> –Hall of Fame broadcaster Ernie Harwell

By the time Ruth retired in 1935, he held the record for home runs in a season (60) and in a career (714), and his .690 career slugging percentage will likely never be topped. When he hit 60 homers in 1927, his total was more than each of the seven other AL teams.

Soon other sluggers followed. Through the 1920s and 1930s, Lou Gehrig of the Yankees, Jimmie Foxx of the Philadelphia Athletics, and Mel Ott of the New York Giants were hitting home runs in bunches.

Yankees teammates Mickey Mantle (left) and Roger Maris captivated baseball fans with their 1961 home run race.

In the 1940s, Ted Williams of the Red Sox and Joe DiMaggio of the Yankees became the dominant sluggers. Ralph Kiner of the Pittsburgh Pirates and Hank Greenberg of the Detroit Tigers also were great power hitters. In the 1950s, two of baseball's greatest all-around players, Willie Mays of the Giants and Mickey Mantle of the Yankees, emerged. Each hit more than 50 homers in a season twice.

In 1961 a pair of Yankees excited the nation. Mantle and Roger Maris gained attention by threatening to break Ruth's season mark of 60 home runs. By September, Maris had the edge. Maris had 51, and Mantle was injured. A private man, Maris hated the media attention and the pressure that came with the home run race. But he wanted the record. On September 26, Maris hit No. 60. On October 1, in the final game of the season, he hit No. 61.

Since then, other great home run hitters have excited fans and made history.

On April 8, 1974, Henry Aaron of the Atlanta Braves hit his 715th home run. That broke Ruth's career record. Aaron's quest also came with pressure. As a black player, he received death threats in 1973 and '74 as he approached the record of Ruth, who was white. Aaron finished his career with 755 home runs.

Another home run race captured the nation's attention in 1998. The St. Louis Cardinals' Mark McGwire and the Chicago Cubs' Sammy Sosa each blew past Maris's record of 61. Sosa hit 66. McGwire hit 70. Those feats, however, proved to be tainted. Both players were accused of using banned performance-enhancing drugs (PEDs). That time is known as the "steroid era." Many players tested positive or were accused of using drugs in the quest to get stronger, hit more home runs, and sign richer contracts.

That was true of Barry Bonds, who was accused of using steroids. Bonds was a star player for the Pirates and the San Francisco Giants in the 1980s and early 1990s. Yet in his late 30s, with the help of PEDs, he starting having some of the most dominant hitting seasons in baseball history. The most famous of those was in 2001, when Bonds hit a record 73 home runs. On August 8, 2007, he hit his 756th home run to pass Aaron. Bonds retired in 2007 with a record 762 homers.

Baseball cracked down on PEDs after that. Today's players are tested more often and punished more harshly than in the steroid era. And yet a new generation of sluggers such as Giancarlo Stanton and Aaron Judge continued to whack home runs into the outfield stands. In 2017 major league players set a record for most total home runs in a season (6,105). When the Houston Astros beat the Los Angeles Dodgers in that year's World Series, the games featured multiple comebacks fueled by home runs. No lead was safe. Almost 100 years after Babe Ruth thrilled fans, the home run is still king.

Slugger Aaron Judge continued a long tradition of Yankees power hitters upon joining the club in 2016.

"That's what Major League Baseball wants," said Astros pitcher Dallas Keuchel. "They want that exciting, two home run lead, and then they come back and hit another home run, and everybody's still watching. That's what they want. That's what they're getting."

CHAPTER 4

BASEBALL'S BIGGEST STAGE: THE WORLD SERIES

Game 5 of the 2017 World Series had a bit of everything. The Los Angeles Dodgers and Houston Astros combined for seven home runs. Each team used seven pitchers in a 5-hour, 17-minute game. And in the end, the Astros won 13–12 in 10 innings at Houston's Minute Maid Park.

The game had no shortage of action. The Dodgers went up 3–0 in the first inning. The Astros tied it 4–4 in the fourth. Both teams scored three runs in the fifth. Houston built a three-run lead going into the

Carlos Correa blasts a two-run home run for the Astros in Game 5 of the 2017 World Series.

ninth, but the Dodgers tied the score. Finally, with two outs in the bottom of the 10th, the Astros scored the winning run.

The game was called an "instant classic" by a writer who was covering his 42nd straight Series. Astros shortstop Carlos Correa said the game was so intense that he felt as if he were going to "have a heart attack."

It turned out to be the wildest game of a wild Series. The Astros eventually won in seven games to claim their first Series trophy.

Each year, every team begins spring training with the hope of reaching the World Series. It is baseball's biggest stage. Only two of 30 teams make it. The Fall Classic, as it's known, matches the AL winner against the NL winner to determine the major league champion.

It's a major challenge just to reach the Series. Teams need a great regular season, then must come through their league playoffs to earn a spot. For some teams, such as the Astros, that's rare. Founded in 1962, the team had reached the Fall Classic just once before winning in 2017. For others, such as the New York Yankees and St. Louis Cardinals, it's part of their tradition. Through 2017, the Yankees had reached the

Pitcher Charlie Morton lifts catcher Brian McCann after the Astros won the 2017 World Series.

Series 40 times and won 27; the Cardinals had made 19 appearances and won 11 titles. When a team finally wins after decades of failure, it's one of the biggest sports stories of a year. Just ask the Astros, Cubs (in 2016), White Sox (2005), Red Sox (2004), or Angels (2002).

> " You don't ever think of playing in Game 3 or 4 or 5. As a kid, you're always playing in Game 7."
>
> –Astros outfielder George Springer

World Series drama can play out over a week or longer if the best-of-seven format goes to a seventh game. That has happened 39 times through 2017. Then, like football's Super Bowl or college basketball's national championship game, it's down to a do-or-die situation. Every pitch and every play are meaningful.

Almost every kid who plays the game dreams about playing in a Game 7. Kids play it out in back yards and diamonds across the country.

"You don't ever think of playing in Game 3 or 4 or 5," said Astros outfielder George Springer. "As a kid, you're always playing in Game 7."

The World Series began in 1903. That year, Barney Dreyfuss, owner of the Pittsburgh Pirates, invited the winner of the three-year-old AL to play a best-of-nine

World Series. The Boston Americans (now the Red Sox) beat the Pirates five games to three.

The next year, the NL champion New York Giants refused to play the AL champion. They believed the upstart AL was inferior. The standoff didn't last, though, and the two leagues reached an agreement to play a World Series every fall. The only time that hasn't happened since 1904 was in 1994. A players' strike in August wiped out that postseason.

Outside of 1994, the darkest moment in Series history came in 1919. That year, eight members of the Chicago White Sox, including star outfielder "Shoeless" Joe Jackson, were accused of making a deal with gamblers to lose to the Cincinnati Reds. The Reds indeed won, and all eight Chicago players were banned from baseball. The incident is known as the Black Sox scandal.

For most of its history, the World Series has featured a best-of-seven schedule. Since 1905, that format was used in all but three years. Best-of-nine series were adopted for the 1919–21 seasons to generate more money from ticket sales. But the Series returned to best-of-seven in 1922.

Through 1968 the teams with the best regular-season records from each league went straight to the

New York Yankees pitcher Don Larson throws a perfect game against the Brooklyn Dodgers in Game 5 of the 1956 World Series.

Series. Since 1969, teams have had to qualify through a playoff system.

With so much focus each fall on the World Series, participating players have achieved fame for heroics or mistakes.

Heroics have come in many ways. In 1956 Yankees pitcher Don Larsen threw the only perfect game in Series history to beat the Brooklyn Dodgers. Four years later, Pittsburgh's Bill Mazeroski hit a home run in the bottom of the ninth inning of Game 7 to give the Pirates a walk-off World Series win over the Yankees.

In 1993 Joe Carter ended another World Series with a home run. The Toronto Blue Jays slugger blasted a homer in the bottom of the ninth of Game 6 to secure the win over the Philadelphia Phillies.

And then there was Willie Mays. Game 1 of the 1954 World Series was tied 2–2 in the eighth inning. Cleveland's Vic Wertz blasted a deep fly ball into the outfield. With two men on base, Cleveland was certain to take the lead. Instead, Mays, the Giants' center fielder, raced back. His sensational over-the-shoulder catch saved the game, and the Giants went on to beat Cleveland. Since then, fans have loved to compare any great catch to Mays's stunning grab.

Of course, the Series has seen its blunders, too. In 1912 Giants center fielder Fred Snodgrass dropped a fly ball in the 10th inning of a deciding game against the Red Sox. The error allowed Boston to score two runs to win the game. In 1925 Washington Senators shortstop Roger Peckinpaugh committed eight errors overall. Three of the errors led to losses that allowed the Pirates to win in seven games. And then there was 1986. The Red Sox were just one out from winning the Series in Game 6. That's when first baseman Bill Buckner let a ground ball go through his legs. The

> Joe Carter celebrates after his walk-off home run gave
> the Toronto Blue Jays the 1993 World Series title.

New York Mets won that game and the next. It was a
heartbreaking loss for Sox fans but another memorable
moment in World Series history.

CHAPTER 5

BREAKING THE COLOR LINE

Jackie Robinson was about to make history. No black player had taken part in a major league game in more than 60 years. Robinson was going to change that.

As he waited before the season's first game at Brooklyn's Ebbets Field on April 15, 1947, Robinson was asked by a reporter if he was nervous. Was he feeling any butterflies?

"Not a one," said Robinson. "I wish I could say I did because then maybe I'd have an alibi if I don't do so good."

It turned out he didn't need an alibi. The Brooklyn Dodgers' first baseman scored a run in a 5–3 victory

 Jackie Robinson's arrival to MLB helped other parts of society move toward integration, too.

over the Boston Braves. Yet it wasn't so much what Robinson did on the field. Just being on the field was what was important.

Black people faced brutal discrimination and were treated poorly throughout the country. For Robinson to make it to the top in the country's most popular sport marked a huge milestone. It showed that integration was possible.

Technically, black players were never officially banned by Major League Baseball. However, an unwritten rule had the same effect. Beginning in the 1880s, teams simply did not sign black players.

Dodgers executive Branch Rickey decided to change that. He knew there were great black players competing in the all-black Negro Leagues. So, if a black player could help his team, Rickey decided there was no reason not to sign him.

Robinson's ability in the Negro Leagues was well known. But Rickey knew the first black player would need to be both good at baseball and mentally strong enough to endure the hostility from some players and fans. Robinson proved to be that player. His example opened the door for more black players to sign with major league teams.

> Jackie Robinson became known for his speedy base
> running.

Larry Doby came next. He signed with the Cleveland Indians on July 5, 1947. Later that month, Hank Thompson and Willard Brown joined the St. Louis Browns. In 1949 Monte Irvin played for the New York Giants. By 1960 the color line had been broken on every major league team.

Robinson had opened the door. He also had set a high standard on the field. He was an exciting and daring player who could hit, field, and run. Two years after his debut, Robinson was voted the NL's MVP. And in 1962, he was elected to the Baseball Hall of Fame.

Robinson once said, "A life is not important except in the impact it has on other lives." His life had an enormous impact. He was a pioneer for African-American opportunity and became one of the leaders of the civil rights movement.

> "Robinson's success on the baseball diamond was a symbol of the promise of a racially integrated society," said professor Peter Dreier of Occidental College. "He did more than change the way baseball is played and who plays it. His actions on and off the diamond helped pave the way for America to confront its racial hypocrisy."

Today Robinson's No. 42 is retired by every team in the majors. April 15 is celebrated in the major leagues as Jackie Robinson Day.

That just shows how far the game has come.

44

Moses Fleetwood Walker was the first black player to compete at the major league level. That was in 1884, when the American Association was considered a major league. Walker was a catcher for the Toledo Blue Stockings. Later that year his brother Welday joined him.

But the Walkers' careers were cut short. Cap Anson, one of the greatest players of his time, didn't believe black athletes should be allowed to play professional baseball. Anson led a movement to bar black players from organized baseball. That ban lasted until Robinson's 1947 debut.

In the years after the Walkers played, black players would barnstorm across the country, playing games against black and white teams. Starting in 1920, the best black players played in organized, high-level leagues such as the Negro National League and Negro American League. Teams such as the Kansas City Monarchs, Homestead Grays (of Washington, DC), Newark Eagles, Detroit Stars, and Birmingham Black Barons competed for many years.

The players who played in those leagues became legends, too. Outfielders "Cool Papa" Bell and Oscar Charleston, catcher Josh Gibson, third baseman Judy

Johnson, pitcher-outfielder Martin Dihigo, shortstop John Henry "Pop" Lloyd, and first baseman Buck Leonard were exciting to watch. Pitchers such as Satchel Paige and Leon Day dominated opponents. All were elected to the Baseball Hall of Fame.

Though most never were given the chance to compete in major league games against the best white players of their era, black players impressed many white stars in barnstorming exhibition games.

Gibson was called the Negro Leagues' greatest hitter. It's believed he hit nearly 800 home runs. In a game at Yankee Stadium, he was credited with hitting a 580-foot home run.

"Josh was a better power hitter than Babe Ruth, Ted Williams, or anybody else I've ever seen," said Negro Leagues pitcher and manager Alonzo Boone. "Anything he touched was hit hard."

Gibson, however, never had the opportunity to play Major League Baseball. Only when Rickey signed Robinson to the Dodgers did that change. But Rickey didn't want praise for that decision.

"I do not deserve any recognition from anybody on the Robinson thing," he said. "It is a terrible commentary on all of us that a part of us should not concede equal rights to everybody to earn a living."

Josh Gibson tries to avoid the tag at home plate during
the Negro Leagues' East-West All-Star Game in Chicago.

CHAPTER 6

CHEATING

In the early 1990s, Albert Belle was one of Major League Baseball's best power hitters. The Cleveland Indians outfielder hit 34 home runs in 1992. He followed with seasons of 38, 36, and a career-best 50 in 1995. Over 12 seasons, Belle hit 381 home runs.

Yet it wasn't just muscle that helped Belle hit the ball into the outfield seats. In 1994 Belle was caught using a corked bat.

A corked bat is a regular wooden bat that has been hollowed out at the end and filled with cork. Because cork is lighter, a player can swing the bat faster and create greater distance on hits. Players also believe the cork in the bat provides a "trampoline effect," which helps launch the ball farther. It is illegal to use a corked bat.

 Albert Belle's accomplishments on the field were overshadowed by his attempts to cheat.

49

On July 15, 1994, White Sox manager Gene Lamont suspected Belle was using an illegal bat. He alerted the umpires. The umpires took Belle's bat and locked it up in their room at the ballpark, planning to inspect it later.

But Belle's teammate, pitcher Jason Grimsley, decided to help Belle. Grimsley and the rest of the Indians knew Belle used a corked bat. In fact, all of his bats at the time were corked. They also knew he would be suspended if he were caught. So Grimsley crawled up into the ceiling of the Indians' clubhouse during the game and made his way over to the umpires' room. He dropped down through the ceiling, replaced Belle's bat with a normal bat, and escaped.

Umpires discovered the switch, and major league officials demanded the Indians give up Belle's bat. They did. When it was examined, it indeed was corked. Belle was suspended for seven games.

In the playoffs a year later, Belle hit a long home run against the Boston Red Sox, and his bat again was taken by the umpires. When it was examined later, there was no cork. The next day, Belle yelled out to the Red Sox and pointed to his biceps. He said his home run was powered by muscle, not cork.

"I was mad because they accused me of cheating," he said.

Baseball has a long history of players trying to get an edge by bending or breaking the rules. In fact, former Chicago Cubs first

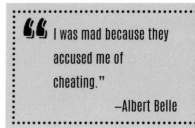

" I was mad because they accused me of cheating."
—Albert Belle

baseman Mark Grace once said, "If you're not cheating, you're not trying." Grace's own teammate, Sammy Sosa, was caught cheating in 2003. When he made contact with the ball during one at-bat, his bat broke, and the illegal cork inside was exposed.

There has long been a debate about stealing another team's signs. This has been going on since the 1800s. There are no rules against watching a third-base coach and figuring out what his signs are. But using technology to steal signs is prohibited.

In the early 1950s, the New York Giants set up a telescope in center field to steal the signs of the opposing catcher. A signal could then be sent to the Giants' dugout and a sign could be sent to the batter so he would know what type of pitch was coming. In 2017 the Boston Red Sox were caught stealing signs and relaying details to their players using Apple watches.

Pitchers also try to get an advantage against hitters. By cutting, marking, or putting mud or a slippery substance on the baseball, pitchers can make the ball move unexpectedly.

Whitey Ford was a Hall of Fame pitcher for the New York Yankees in the 1950s and '60s. He said after he retired that he used to cut the baseball with a ring on his finger. He also put substances such as baby oil or turpentine on the ball. Gaylord Perry, who won 314 games in a 22-year career that ended in 1983, often was accused of throwing illegal pitches. In fact, he said he liked having that reputation because it made hitters look for his "spitball" even if he didn't throw it.

Some pitchers have been caught cheating. Umpires found Rick Honeycutt with a thumbtack in his glove in 1980. Joe Niekro had a nail file in his pocket in a 1987 game. Either could be used to scuff the ball.

A different kind of cheating occurred in 1919, when eight members of the White Sox, who became known as the Black Sox, were paid by gamblers to intentionally lose World Series games. All eight were banned from baseball for life. It has been called "the greatest scandal in baseball history."

Gaylord Perry was one of many pitchers over the years caught using foreign substances to affect the ball.

Pete Rose, a sure Hall of Famer, was banned from the game in 1989. As a player, Rose had a record 4,256 hits. But as manager of the Cincinnati Reds, he was caught betting on baseball, which is against the rules. If a player bets on a game, the thinking goes, he could intentionally help his team lose to make money for himself or others. Because of this, voters have refused to elect Rose to the Hall.

Perhaps the most widespread type of cheating occurred during baseball's "steroid era." From the late 1980s into the early 2000s, multiple star players were caught or accused of using PEDs such as steroids. Those substances allow players to work out more intensely and more often. That allows them to gain strength unfairly. Hitters could hit the ball farther and pitchers could throw harder. Such stars as all-time home run leader Barry Bonds, Mark McGwire, Jose Canseco, Roger Clemens, Sammy Sosa, Jason Giambi, and Rafael Palmeiro were implicated, admitted using PEDs, or tested positive for their use.

Since then, baseball's drug-testing policy has been made stricter. Still, many believe players will always look for an edge, even one that goes against the rules. More success leads to more fame and bigger contracts. To some players, the risk is worth the reward.

Mark McGwire hit a record 70 home runs for the Cardinals in 1998, but it later came out that he was using PEDs.

CHAPTER 7

GREAT MANAGERS, DIFFERENT STYLES

In parts of nine seasons in the major leagues, Bruce Bochy was a bit player. The backup catcher had almost as many career strikeouts (177) as hits (192). His batting average was a paltry .239. He spent far more time on the bench than on the field. "My skills were limited," he said. "I understood that." Yet someday, Bochy might be elected to the Baseball Hall of Fame.

After retiring as a player in 1988, Bochy became a manager. In his first 23 years of managing the San Diego Padres and then the San Francisco Giants, his

Bruce Bochy led the San Francisco Giants to three World Series wins in five years from 2010 to 2014.

teams made the playoffs four times and won four NL pennants. Most notably, under Bochy the Giants won three World Series in five seasons.

Often, Bochy guided championship teams that weren't considered among the most talented. Yet he consistently got the most out of his roster. He proved to be a master at managing his starting pitching rotation and bullpen. In a 2015 poll of 50 baseball executives, scouts, and coaches, Bochy was selected as the No. 1 manager in the big leagues.

His leadership and communication skills are strengths. He rarely criticizes a player in public and supports any player who plays hard. Pitcher Tim Hudson once compared him to Hall of Fame manager Bobby Cox, saying both motivate and support their players. "They'll fight for you," said Hudson. His former teammate and third-base coach Tim Flannery said Bochy "has great compassion, but he holds people accountable."

"I want to treat players the way I want to be treated," said Bochy.

> I want to treat players the way I want to be treated."
> —San Francisco Giants manager Bruce Bochy

Managing a team isn't easy. From the start of spring training until the season's end, a manager is in charge of everything. He decides the lineup and when to change pitchers or pinch hit. He decides where to play fielders and when to bunt, steal, or call a hit-and-run. He has to deal with a variety of personalities. The manager needs to know how to discipline a player one day and motivate him the next.

While Bochy's strengths are pitching and people skills, other managers have won with far different styles. Joe Maddon is another respected manager, having led the Chicago Cubs to the 2016 World Series championship. Maddon began using computers as a minor league manager. While Bochy often makes moves based on his instincts, Maddon often makes decisions based on computer analytics. He was an early believer in the importance of on-base percentage over batting average. He also was a pioneer in defensive shifts. In a shift, fielders are positioned according to where batters have historically hit the ball.

Over the years, managers have taken many routes to success.

In the 1970s and '80s, two Hall of Fame–bound managers, Whitey Herzog and Earl Weaver, had far different styles.

Orioles manager Earl Weaver won four AL pennants and one World Series in 17 seasons in Baltimore.

Herzog loved speed. His lineups were filled with players who slapped singles and doubles, stole bases, and bunted. His teams were similar to those that played in the "dead-ball era." His St. Louis Cardinals and Kansas City Royals teams played "Whiteyball." Speed, defense, and pitching were the way to win in his home ballparks. St. Louis and Kansas City had big ballparks with fast, artificial surfaces.

Weaver loved power. His Baltimore Orioles lineups were filled with slower players who hit home runs. His teams rarely stole bases or bunted. Weaver said his formula for winning was "pitching, defense, and three-run homers."

Some successful managers have been loud personalities who ruled their teams with iron fists. Leo Durocher was called "Leo the Lip" for his talkative nature. His combative style with umpires and players was a trademark of his managerial career, which lasted from 1939 to 1973. He once was suspended for a year because of his behavior. Billy Martin, a former scrappy infielder, became a scrappy manager in 1969. He argued with umpires and fought his own players and owners. Martin's teams won, but he often quickly wore out his welcome.

Connie Mack (center) watches his Philadelphia Athletics alongside two assistants during the 1920s.

Their styles were far different from that of Connie Mack, who took over the Philadelphia Athletics in 1901 and won five World Series championships and nine AL pennants in 50 seasons. Mack was called "the grand old gentleman of the game." He wore a suit and tie

in the dugout. He was known as a kind, soft-spoken manager who treated his players well. Mack holds major league managerial records for wins (3,731), losses (3,948), and years managed (53). He is No. 3 in World Series titles, with five. Casey Stengel and Joe McCarthy won seven each with the New York Yankees.

CHAPTER 8

THE STARS COME OUT

At first, it was called the "Game of the Century." The match between the greatest players in the American and National leagues was supposed to be just a one-time event. Chicago was the site of the World's Fair in 1933. *Chicago Tribune* sports editor Arch Ward pitched the idea of an all-star game as part of the Fair and a celebration of the city's 100th anniversary.

Ward believed a game between the best players in baseball would be exciting for fans. It also would be a way to revive interest in the sport. In the midst of the Great Depression, attendance had declined. People lost jobs and had little money for tickets. Yet Ward was

 Giants ace Carl Hubbell (left) shakes hands with Athletics pitcher Lefty Grove at the 1933 All-Star Game.

so certain that his idea of an all-star game would succeed that he offered to have any financial losses taken out of his paycheck.

Ward was correct. On July 6, 1933, a sellout crowd of nearly 50,000 fans turned out to Comiskey Park. They saw the AL stars beat the NL 4–2. Two national radio networks broadcast the game. The event produced a profit of $45,000, which was donated to a charity for retired players.

Fans across the nation voted for the players they wanted in the game. Outfielder Babe Ruth and first baseman Lou Gehrig of the New York Yankees, shortstop Joe Cronin of the Washington Senators, and Charlie Gehringer of the Detroit Tigers were among the AL starters. Outfielder Chuck Klein of the Philadelphia Phillies, second baseman Frankie Frisch and third baseman Pepper Martin of the St. Louis Cardinals, and first baseman Bill Terry of the New York Giants were in the NL lineup. Connie Mack managed the AL team, with John McGraw guiding the NL. Sixteen players who participated would go on to be elected to the Baseball Hall of Fame.

Ruth's two-run home run in the third inning gave his team a 3–0 lead. His teammate, Lefty Gomez,

> Manager Connie Mack (in black) poses with the 1933 AL All-Star Team.

started and pitched a scoreless three innings to get the win.

"Wasn't it swell, an All-Star Game?" said Ruth. "Wasn't it a great idea? And we won it, besides."

Baseball commissioner Kenesaw Mountain Landis called it a "grand show" that should be continued. Baseball's owners agreed. They voted to make the All-Star Game an annual event. It would be played in a different city each season. It now is played on a Tuesday each July.

Through the years, the All-Star Game produced some of the game's most memorable moments.

AL teammates congratulate Ted Williams after his ninth-inning home run in the 1941 All-Star Game.

In 1941 22-year-old Red Sox outfielder Ted Williams hit a three-run home run in the ninth inning to give the AL a come-from-behind 7–5 victory. Williams was so excited that he clapped while galloping around the bases. Years later he called it one of his favorite memories. "I've never been so happy," he said.

In 1970 the game was tied with two outs in the bottom of the 12th inning. Then Pete Rose of the Cincinnati Reds dashed home from second base on a single. The throw from center field to Cleveland

Indians catcher Ray Fosse arrived before Rose did, but Rose lowered his shoulder and ran into Fosse. The ball came loose, Rose scored, and the NL won 5–4. Rose was criticized for his aggressive play, which resulted in a shoulder injury to Fosse, but he never apologized.

In 2007 Ichiro Suzuki of the Seattle Mariners hit the first inside-the-park home run in All-Star Game history. With a runner aboard, the speedy Ichiro hit a ball off the right-field wall. It took a crazy bounce away from the outfielder. The home run gave the AL a 2–1 lead on the way to a 5–4 victory.

Perhaps the lowest All-Star moment occurred in 2002, when the game at Milwaukee's new Miller Park ended in a 7–7 tie after 11 innings. The teams ran out of pitchers. Fans at the game were so angry they booed baseball commissioner Bud Selig, who was in his hometown. They also chanted, "Bud must go!"

Since the first game in 1933, the All-Star format has changed several times. When fans in Cincinnati stuffed the ballot box to vote eight Reds into the NL starting lineup in 1957, baseball commissioner Ford Frick took the vote away from fans. Two years later, baseball decided there would be two All-Star Games each year in a bid to raise more money. But, after the 1962 games, baseball returned to just one game.

Pregame festivities included a giant flag and an Air Force flyover at the 2014 All-Star Game at Target Field in Minneapolis.

In 1970 fan voting was resumed to spark more interest. In 2003, the year after the tie, it was decided the winning league would receive home-field advantage in the World Series. Selig said it was a "fresh, bold, creative" idea to spark more interest. That idea was erased in 2017.

The annual game between AL and NL stars remains a big event, but it has expanded to include other features. Over several days, a Fan Fest in the host city allows fans to view memorabilia and take part in interactive exhibits. A Futures Game is held between the best minor league prospects. There's a celebrity softball game, too. A home-run derby is held the day before the actual game.

CHAPTER 9

CHARACTERS AND CRAZINESS

Rube Waddell was one of baseball's greatest pitchers in the early 1900s. The Philadelphia Athletics ace had a legendary fastball and curve as well as great control. In 1904 he struck out 349 batters, a season record that stood until 1965. His manager, Connie Mack, said Waddell had the best stuff of any pitcher he had ever seen.

Yet Waddell is known as much for his colorful personality as his Hall of Fame career. During games he would talk to fans and opposing players. He always looked as if he was having fun. Wherever he played, attendance increased. "He would put on a show," said Dan O'Brien, who wrote a screenplay about Waddell.

 Rube Waddell played for five teams between 1897 and 1910.

In a sport that has had hundreds of wacky characters, Waddell is hard to beat as the craziest of them all. He might leave in the middle of games to go fishing or chase a fire truck that had sped past the park. Sometimes he was late to games because he had stopped to play marbles with kids. In the offseason, he wrestled alligators and played semipro football. Several times while playing exhibition games against college teams, he waved his teammates off the field and struck out the side. Writers at the time called him "eccentric," a "screwball," or "nutsy."

More than any other major American sport, baseball has the time for its characters to express themselves. The season is 162 games long. Frequent travel and long hours before, during, and after games allow players to talk and kill time.

"There's an exorbitant amount of wasted time spent at the ballpark," said Joe Maddon, who has managed the Chicago Cubs and Tampa Bay Rays.

Pitcher Moe Drabowsky spent a lot of time in bullpens during his 17-year career from 1956 to 1972. He became famous for his pranks. He would order pizza or call overseas from the bullpen phone. He often gave teammates the "hot foot" by attaching a book of matches to their shoes and lighting it. He loved snakes and would hide them in teammates' lockers. He put goldfish in the opposing team's water cooler.

Sometimes, a team takes on the personality of its cast of characters. That was the case with the St. Louis Cardinals of the early 1930s. They were known as the "Gashouse Gang." Players such as brothers Dizzy and Paul Dean, Frankie Frisch, Leo Durocher, Pepper Martin, and Joe "Ducky" Medwick played hard and often had dirty uniforms (like auto mechanics in a gas station) from sliding and diving. Players often played pranks. They even formed a musical group, Pepper Martin's Mudcat Band. Durocher said they were a scrappy group that was good at having fun and fighting.

> " We fought among ourselves, but we stuck together if anyone picked on us. There was a fight every day...with each other or the other ballclub."
>
> —Leo Durocher of the Cardinals' "Gashouse Gang"

"We fought among ourselves, but we stuck together if anyone picked on us," he said. "There was a fight every day...with each other or the other ballclub."

Mark Fidrych poses with the real Big Bird ahead of a
game against the New York Yankees.

Herman "Germany" Schaefer was a fine infielder for the Detroit Tigers in the early 1900s. He gained fame by the quirky things he would do. As a pinch hitter he once hit a game-winning home run, then slid into every base on his trot around the bags. He once walked to the plate in rubber boots and a raincoat when the umpires allowed the game to continue in a downpour. He was ejected. In another game, Schaefer stole second base, then stole first. His goal was to force the catcher to make a bad throw that would allow a teammate to score from third.

Some players are superstitious and follow routines that become familiar to fans. In 1976, the Tigers' Mark "The Bird" Fidrych caught the nation's attention because of his pitching and resemblance to Big Bird on *Sesame Street*. He was tall and skinny with bushy yellow hair. While pitching, Fidrych would talk to the ball, point to home plate to show it where it needed to go, circle the mound after each out, and drop to his knees to groom the dirt with his bare hands.

Equally eccentric was relief pitcher Turk Wendell. During an 11-year career that ended in 2004, he had multiple routines. He always jumped over the foul line. He squatted on the mound until his catcher squatted.

He drew three crosses in the dirt behind the mound. He waved to the center fielder before his first pitch. He didn't wear socks. And he brushed his teeth between innings. "If I find something that works for me, I stay with it, no matter how crazy it may seem," he said.

Perhaps baseball's most quotable character was Yogi Berra. Berra was a Hall of Fame catcher for the New York Yankees. He had a way of speaking that left teammates and reporters laughing or scratching their heads. Among the quotes attributed to Berra:

"You can observe a lot by just watching."

"When you come to a fork in the road, take it."

"A nickel ain't worth a dime anymore."

"No one goes there nowadays. It's too crowded."

"It gets late early out there."

"Why buy good luggage? You only use it when you travel."

In addition to his famous phrases, Yogi Berra won a record 10 World Series, all with the New York Yankees.

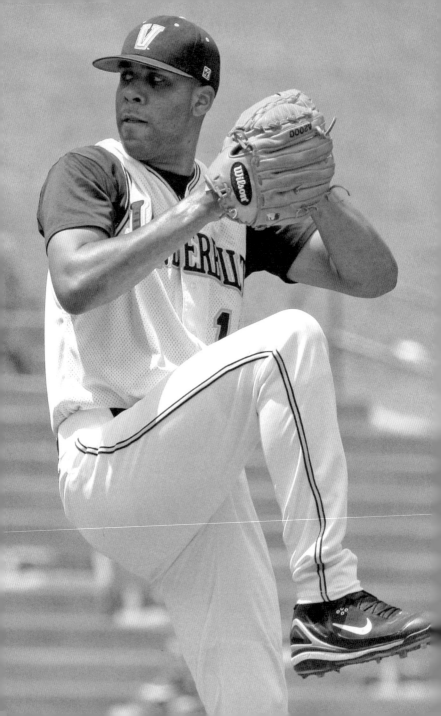

CHAPTER 10

BLUE CHIPPERS AND NO-CHIPPERS

With the first pick of the Major League Baseball draft in June 2007, the Tampa Bay Rays selected pitcher David Price of Vanderbilt University. It wasn't a surprise. Price, a tall, athletic left-hander, had a great fastball and slider. He had been projected for years as a star. He received a six-year deal worth $11.25 million. That included a $5.6 million signing bonus.

About three months earlier in Venezuela, a short, skinny 16-year-old named Jose Altuve showed up to a Houston Astros tryout camp. He was turned away. Scouts saw nothing but his size. Altuve returned to try again the next day. This time they allowed him to

 Baseball scouts had high expectations for David Price even during his college days at Vanderbilt University.

participate. Once they saw his skills, they signed him to a $15,000 contract.

Price and Altuve became stars yet traveled far different paths. Price has been a 20-game winner and a Cy Young Award winner as the best pitcher in the AL, and he has led his league in strikeouts and ERA. Altuve, at 5 feet 6, is the shortest player in the majors but is a three-time AL batting champion. Through 2017 he had a .316 career batting average and four seasons of 200 hits or more. Nothing could top his 2017 season. Altuve was his league's MVP and the Astros won their first World Series championship.

As Altuve and many others have shown, baseball scouting isn't an exact science. When scouts first looked at him, they didn't give him a chance. He hopes his story encourages young players and is a lesson for scouts not to judge a player by his appearance.

"Whoever plays well should have the right to play," Altuve said.

While some players such as Price are tagged as blue-chip prospects (a term for the best), not all are sure things. In 2013 Stanford pitcher Mark Appel was drafted first overall by the Astros. Like Price, Appel was considered a can't-miss player. Yet he missed. Injuries

Few scouts expected Jose Altuve to make the major leagues when he was younger.

and ineffectiveness had kept him from reaching the big leagues through 2017.

In 2002 the Pittsburgh Pirates drafted pitcher Bryan Bullington No. 1 overall. But he appeared in just 26 major league games with a 1–9 career record. Other famous misses among first overall draft picks include infielder Matt Bush by the San Diego Padres in 2004 (he eventually made it as a relief pitcher) and

> **Albert Pujols hit at least .300 with 100 RBIs and 30 home runs in each of his first 10 seasons with the Cardinals.**

pitcher Brien Taylor by the New York Yankees in 1991. He never played a big-league game.

Hall of Fame manager Tommy Lasorda of the Los Angeles Dodgers has said that baseball scouts have a difficult job.

"Projecting (talent) is a craft," he said. "It's the art of looking at some 17- or 18-year-old kid and determining how good he will be when he's 23 or 24, when his body has filled out and he's had a few years of minor league experience under his belt."

Lasorda said scouts can be fooled because some players mature faster. They look dominating until others catch up. Or, scouts might see a talented player with little drive, or a less-talented athlete with incredible drive.

Albert Pujols was an NL Rookie of the Year and a three-time MVP for the St. Louis Cardinals, and he has more than 600 career home runs and 3,000 career hits. In 1999, however, Pujols wasn't drafted until the 13th round. One scout's report on Pujols said he had a "heavy, bulky body." He predicted Pujols would have weight problems and would chase bad pitches. He also questioned his power.

In 1987 the Astros drafted catcher Craig Biggio in the first round. He also played second base and all three outfield spots during his 20-year Hall of Fame career. Biggio retired with 3,060 hits, 291 home runs, and 414 stolen bases. Yet one scout reported Biggio didn't have a major league bat or power.

In 2016 the Baseball Hall of Fame class consisted of a blue chipper and no-chipper. Ken Griffey Jr. was the first choice in the 1987 draft. He became one of the best players of his era. Known as "The Kid," the Seattle Mariners star had power and speed and was a terrific outfielder. A year later, the Dodgers selected catcher Mike Piazza in the 62nd round, the 1,390th choice. Piazza developed into perhaps the best-hitting catcher of all time. He had a .308 career batting average with 427 home runs in a 16-year career.

Griffey was the first top overall draft choice to make the Hall of Fame. Piazza is the lowest pick to have been enshrined. Piazza passed pitcher John Smoltz as the lowest drafted player in the Hall of Fame. In 2015 Smoltz was elected after being taken in the 22nd round of the 1985 draft by the Detroit Tigers. Piazza, like Smoltz and Altuve, surpassed all expectations.

Altuve has great physical skills as a fielder, base runner, and hitter. He also has surprising power. But there are other qualities the baseball scouts missed when they saw him on the first day of that tryout camp at age 16. His Houston teammates say he's a leader. Teammates follow him.

"The more you get to know him, the greater you think he is," said Astros pitcher Dallas Keuchel. "Because he's not just about this MVP-type talent. He's a leader in the clubhouse. He's a guy who can make

Mike Piazza (left) and Ken Griffey Jr. show off their Hall of Fame plaques.

you laugh at any point in time....You hear about his tryout in Venezuela. That's been well documented. To see the perseverance and work ethic he put into the game, into his job...you see a bunch of guys float toward that."

CHAPTER 11

BASEBALL'S SPREAD AND FUTURE

Baseball is much the same today as it was when Babe Ruth was belting home runs for the Yankees in the 1920s. Three strikes is an out. Four balls is a walk. It's 90 feet between bases. It's 60'6" inches from the top of the pitcher's mound to home plate. When Mike Trout steps in to bat against Clayton Kershaw in the 21st century, it's still a one-on-one duel like Ruth vs. Walter Johnson a century earlier. The structure and soul of the game haven't changed.

 Mike Trout makes a diving catch for the Los Angeles Angels.

Yet baseball has evolved significantly over the past 100 years. It's not standing still. The sport will continue to move in new directions even while embracing its traditions and history.

Although baseball was born and thrives in the United States, it's now a global game. Baseball is popular in Mexico, Cuba, around the Caribbean, and in several nations in South America. It's big in Japan, South Korea, Taiwan, the Philippines, and Australia. It's growing in Europe, and it's likely to spread even farther.

In 2006 a baseball world championship tournament debuted, the World Baseball Classic (WBC). It's held every three to four years, with many of the greatest players in the world participating. Japan won the first two championships, in 2006 and 2009, with the Dominican Republic winning the third in 2013. The United States won in 2017. In 2013 the qualification round for the tournament was expanded to 16 teams. Since then, such countries as Brazil, the Czech Republic, Thailand, Israel, and Pakistan have participated for the first time. The WBC's popularity, attendance, and TV ratings have improved steadily. Meanwhile, baseball returns in 2020 as an Olympic sport, so it will get even more global exposure.

The global growth of the game has led to far more diverse and talented major league rosters. In 2017 Opening Day rosters had 258 players from outside the 50 US states, a record 29.8 percent of all players. They came from 19 nations and territories. Players such as outfielder Ichiro Suzuki and pitcher Yu Darvish of Japan became stars in the United States. Other international standouts have included pitcher Chan Ho Park and outfielder Shin-Soo Choo of South Korea. Australia has contributed pitchers Grant Balfour and Graeme Lloyd. First baseman Jose Abreu and outfielder Yasiel Puig came from Cuba. Third baseman Edwin Encarnacion, second baseman Robinson Cano, and outfielder Jose Bautista are among the many stars signed out of the Dominican Republic. Second baseman Jose Altuve, first baseman Miguel Cabrera, and pitcher Felix Hernandez are from Venezuela.

Though Japan has its own major leagues, its best players often want to come to the United States. They are eager to play against the world's best players and make more money. American teams get into bidding wars to sign them.

In 2018, young Japanese star Shohei Ohtani, who pitches and plays the outfield, joined the Los Angeles Angels. He picked the Angels over six other teams.

In 2001 Ichiro Suzuki won both the AL Rookie of the Year and MVP awards.

"That has always been my dream," said Ohtani. "To play in the major leagues."

When Ichiro Suzuki signed with the Seattle Mariners in 2001, he was a huge star in Japan. But he wanted more.

"I want to be the first player to show what Japanese batters can do in the major leagues," he said. He won two batting titles and had more than 3,000 hits in the United States.

Baseball has had to change as it has expanded. A century ago, it was the number one sport in America. Now there is no shortage of sports to compete for fans' attention. Many of those sports are played at a much faster pace than baseball. They're more popular with young people. One study showed the average age of a baseball fan is 53, older than for the National Football League (47) and National Basketball Association (37). Part of the problem is baseball is too slow for some. The average game today lasts more than three hours, about a half hour longer than in the 1970s. It's an hour longer than a game in the 1940s.

Baseball commissioner Rob Manfred has talked about the need to speed up the game. Putting in a 20-second clock and forcing the pitcher to throw before it runs out is one idea. Multiple pitching changes, batters stepping out of the box between every pitch, and an increase in the number of strikeouts and walks in recent years also slow games. Manfred says the game must address these issues to stay popular in the 21st century.

"We're also interested in capturing new fans, particularly young fans, and we think that a little focus on pace of game, while always respecting the tradition and history of the game, will always help us with the younger group," he said.

One route to reaching more fans is through technology. MLB's website allows fans to watch games on their TVs, computers, tablets, and smartphones. A Milwaukee Brewers fan, for example, can follow the team during a game, watch highlight videos, check stats and other scores, and buy merchandise while in Milwaukee, Florida, or Tokyo. The service has grown steadily since it was introduced in 2002. Millions of fans now subscribe to MLB.com, and that number is certain to increase as more features are offered. Baseball was the first major sport in the United States to offer games for digital viewing. And minor league games also are available to watch on devices.

As baseball's popularity has expanded around the world, MLB has grown more diverse.

As baseball moves forward, Manfred believes it can change with the times and be marketed in a way to make it as popular as ever. Speeding it up and making it more available are key, he says.

"Baseball has always been generational," said Manfred. "Appropriate use of technology is important to making sure the game gets passed on to the next generation."

SEATTLE
MARINERS

OAKLAND
ATHLETICS

SAN FRANCISCO
GIANTS

COLORADO
ROCKIES

LOS ANGELES
DODGERS

LOS ANGELES
ANGELS

SAN DIEGO
PADRES

ARIZONA
DIAMONDBACKS

TEXAS
RANGERS

HOUSTON
ASTROS

MAJOR LEAGUE BASEBALL MAP

MINNESOTA TWINS

MILWAUKEE BREWERS

TORONTO BLUE JAYS

BOSTON RED SOX

DETROIT TIGERS

CLEVELAND INDIANS

PHILADELPHIA PHILLIES

NEW YORK METS

CHICAGO CUBS

CHICAGO WHITE SOX

PITTSBURGH PIRATES

NEW YORK YANKEES

ANSAS CITY OYALS

ST. LOUIS CARDINALS

CINCINNATI REDS

WASHINGTON NATIONALS

BALTIMORE ORIOLES

ATLANTA BRAVES

TAMPA BAY RAYS

MIAMI MARLINS

TIMELINE

1869

The Cincinnati Red Stockings begin play as the first all-professional baseball team.

1876

The National League (NL) plays its first season.

1901

The American League (AL) plays its first season.

1903

The first World Series is held between Boston Americans (AL) and Pittsburgh Pirates (NL), with Boston winning in eight games.

1919

In what becomes known as the "Black Sox" scandal, eight members of the Chicago White Sox are paid by gamblers to intentionally lose the World Series to the Cincinnati Reds.

1926

The St. Louis Cardinals win their first World Series. In 2011 they won their 11th. No NL team had won more.

1927

The Yankees' Babe Ruth hits a record 60 home runs and leads his team to the World Series.

1947

Jackie Robinson plays his first game with the Brooklyn Dodgers, breaking baseball's unwritten rule that banned black players.

1953

Boston Red Sox outfielder Ted Williams ends the season with a .407 batting average, becoming the last player to hit above .400 for a season.

1958

Major League Baseball reaches the West Coast as the Brooklyn Dodgers and New York Giants move to Los Angeles and San Francisco, respectively.

1961–62

The AL expands to 10 teams, followed by the NL expansion to 10 teams the next year.

1969

Each league adds two more teams. The leagues are also broken into divisions, and a playoff round is added before the World Series to determine each league's champion.

1973

The AL adopts the designated hitter rule, allowing a player to replace the pitcher in the batting order.

1977

The AL expands to 14 teams.

1982

Baltimore Orioles shortstop Cal Ripken Jr. begins his iron man streak that eventually sees him play in a record 2,632 consecutive games.

1993

The NL expands to 14 teams.

1994

A wild-card team and extra round of playoffs are added to the postseason. However, the changes don't go into effect until 1995 because a work stoppage leads to the cancelation of the playoffs.

1997

Interleague play begins during the regular season, allowing AL and NL teams to play one another outside of the World Series.

1998

The major leagues expand to 30 teams, with 16 in the NL and 14 in the NL.

2001

San Francisco Giants slugger Barry Bonds hits a record 73 home runs, although it was later revealed that he did so with the help of PEDs.

2009

The Yankees win their 27th World Series, which is more than twice as many as the next-best team.

2013

The Houston Astros move from the NL to the AL to create two 15-team leagues. Each league consists of three five-team divisions.

2016

The Chicago Cubs win the World Series, ending a 108-year drought since their last championship.

THE WINNERS

NEW YORK YANKEES (AL): 27

The Yankees have played in 40 Series, and they've lost more than any other team has won. But with 27 victories, the Yankees have won more than the next two teams combined. Founded in 1903, the Yankees didn't even get to a Series until 1921. Their first championship came in 1923. Since then they have had several eras of dominance, including winning five championships in a row beginning in 1949.

ST. LOUIS CARDINALS (NL): 11

The Cardinals have won a record 19 NL pennants, and their 11 World Series wins are second only to the Yankees. Three of the Cardinals' championships came from 1942 to 1946. A new generation led by slugger Albert Pujols won two more in 2006 and 2011.

PHILADELPHIA-KANSAS CITY-OAKLAND ATHLETICS (AL): 9

The franchise that started in Philadelphia moved to Kansas City in 1955 and then to Oakland in 1968. The A's won four of their championships in Oakland and five in Philadelphia. Their last win came in 1989, when

they beat the neighboring Giants in a Series delayed by a major earthquake.

BOSTON RED SOX (AL): 8

Though the team has been to 12 Series, it had a long championship drought between its fifth and sixth win. After winning five titles from 1903 to 1918, the Red Sox didn't win another until 2004. But after that 86-year drought, the Sox won three in nine years.

NEW YORK–SAN FRANCISCO GIANTS (NL): 8

The Giants won five titles before moving to San Francisco in 1958 and then didn't win another until 2010. However, behind dominant pitching, the Giants won the World Series again in 2012 and 2014.

* Accurate through the 2017 season.

THE BIG THREE

A collection of top-three performers in various statistics.

MOST CAREER HOME RUNS

1. Barry Bonds: 762
2. Hank Aaron: 755
3. Babe Ruth: 714

MOST SINGLE-SEASON HOME RUNS

1. Barry Bonds: 73
2. Mark McGwire: 70
3. Sammy Sosa: 66

BEST CAREER BATTING AVERAGE

1. Ty Cobb: .366
2. Rogers Hornsby: .358
3. Shoeless Joe Jackson: .356

MOST CAREER STOLEN BASES

1. Rickey Henderson: 1,406
2. Lou Brock: 938
3. Billy Hamilton: 914

MOST CAREER HITS

1. Pete Rose: 4,256
2. Ty Cobb: 4,189
3. Hank Aaron: 3,771

MOST CAREER PITCHING VICTORIES

1. Cy Young: 511
2. Walter Johnson: 417
3. Grover Cleveland Alexander: 373
   Christy Mathewson: 373

MOST CAREER STRIKEOUTS

1. Nolan Ryan: 5,714
2. Randy Johnson: 4,875
3. Roger Clemens: 4,672

MOST CAREER SAVES

1. Mariano Rivera: 652
2. Trevor Hoffman: 601
3. Lee Smith: 478

* Accurate through the 2017 season.

FOR MORE INFORMATION

BOOKS

Kaplan, David. *The Plan: Epstein, Maddon, and the Audacious Blueprint for a Cubs Dynasty*. Chicago: Triumph Books, 2017.

The National Baseball Hall of Fame and Museum. *The Hall: A Celebration of Baseball's Greats*. New York: Little Brown and Co., 2014.

Tygiel, Jules. *Baseball's Great Experiment: Jackie Robinson and His Legacy*. Oxford, NY: Oxford University Press, 2008.

ON THE WEB

Baseball Reference
www.baseball-reference.com

Major League Baseball
www.mlb.com

National Baseball Hall of Fame
www.baseballhall.org

Negro Leagues Baseball Museum
www.nlbm.com

PLACES TO VISIT

NATIONAL BASEBALL HALL OF FAME AND MUSEUM

25 Main Street
Cooperstown, NY 13326
888-425-5663
www.baseballhall.org

The game's greatest players are enshrined in the Hall of Fame. Visitors can tour the museum and learn about the players and baseball history in general through interactive exhibits.

NEGRO LEAGUES BASEBALL MUSEUM

1616 East 18th Street
Kansas City, MO 64108
816-221-1920
www.nlbm.com

Located in Kansas City, which was at the center of the Negro Leagues, this museum honors the great players who were for many years kept out of the major leagues due to their skin color.

SELECT BIBLIOGRAPHY

BOOKS

Carino, Peter. Ed. *Baseball/Literature/Culture: Essays, 2004–2005*. Jefferson, NC: McFarland & Co., 2006.

Editors of Sports Illustrated. *Sports Illustrated: the Story of Baseball*. New York: Time Inc. Books, 2018.

Frommer, Harvey. *The Ultimate Yankee Book*. Salem, MA: Page Street Pub. Co., 2017.

Genovese, George. *A Scout's Report: My 70 Years in Baseball*. Jefferson, NC: McFarland & Company, Inc., Publishers, 2015.

Rampersad, Arnold. *Jackie Robinson: A Biography*. New York: Knopf, 1997.

Sandalow, Brian. *Chicago: America's Best Sports Town*. Mendota Heights: Press Box Books, 2018.

Somers, Kent. *100 Things Cardinals Fans Should Know & Do Before They Die*. Chicago: Triumph Books, 2016.

Wright, Dave. *162-0: Imagine a Season in Which the Twins Never Lose*. Chicago: Triumph Books, 2010.

ONLINE

Cannella, Stephen. "Joe Maddon Has a Vision." Sports Illustrated Vault. 6 Oct. 2008. https://www.si.com/vault/2008/10/06/105740410/joe-maddon-has-a-vision. Accessed 20 Mar. 2018.

Covitz, Randy. "Giants' Madison Bumgarner adds to World Series lore with relief performance." *Kansas City Star*. 29 Oct. 2014. http://www.kansascity.com/sports/mlb/kansas-city-royals/article3462543.html. Accessed 20 Mar. 2018.

"Jackie Robinson." National Baseball Hall of Fame. n.d. https://baseballhall.org/hall-of-famers/robinson-jackie. Accessed 15 Feb. 2018.

Hersh, Philip. "Chicago, Babe Ruth helped put first All-Star Game on the map." *Chicago Tribune*. 11 July 2015. http://www.chicagotribune.com/sports/baseball/ct-flashback-all-star-game-spt-0712-20150710-story.html. Accessed 20 Mar. 2018.

Janes, Chelsea. "A brief history of rule-bending in baseball, which has always been just part of the game." *Washington Post*. 6 Sept. 2017. https://www.washingtonpost.com/news/sports/wp/2017/09/06/a-brief-history-of-rule-bending-in-baseball-which-has-always-been-just-part-of-the-game. Accessed 20 Mar. 2018.

INDEX

ABOUT THE AUTHOR

Doug Williams is a freelance writer and former newspaper editor. Williams has written 11 books about sports. He lives in San Diego, California, with his wife and enjoys hiking, traveling, reading, and spending time with his family. He especially loves watching baseball games and playing catch with his grandson, Blake.